History Raiders

Alien Visitations

Louise Spilsbury

CRABTREE
PUBLISHING COMPANY
WWW.CRABTREEBOOKS.COM

Author: Louise Spilsbury
Editors: Sarah Eason, Jennifer Sanderson, and Janine Deschenes
Proofreader and indexer: Tracey Kelly
Editorial director: Kathy Middleton
Proofreader: Crystal Sikkens
Design: Jessica Moon
Cover design: Katherine Berti
Photo research: Rachel Blount
Prepress and print coordination: Katherine Berti
Consultant: Rupert Matthews

Written, developed, and produced by Calcium

Photo Credits:
t=Top, c=Center, b=Bottom, l= Left, r=Right

Cover: Shutterstock
Inside: NASA: NASA/JPL-Caltech: p. 24; Shutterstock: Agap: p. 8 cl; Artfury: p. 16 cl; WilbeerTh Youu Breakk: p. 12 cl; CrackerClips Stock Media: pp. 21, 29 tr; Dabarti CGI: pp. 24 tl, 25; Digital Storm: pp. 3 & throughout; Ducu59us: p. 18; Fotos593: p. 9; HUT Design: p. 16; John Kershner: p. 9; Ktsdesign: p. 12 tl; Martial Red: p. 20 cl; Marzolino: p. 14; Merlin74: p. 6; Jurik Peter: pp. 5, 27; Photobank gallery: pp. 15, 16 tl, 29 bl; Sarmiento Photography: p. 22; SSSCCC: pp. 19, 28 bl; Sviluppo: pp. 7, 8 tl; YummyBuum: p. 24 cl; Zef Art: p. 11; Albert Ziganshin: pp. 4, 20 tl; Zschnepf: p. 10; Wikimedia Commons: Kevin Gill from Nashua, NH, United States: p. 26; NASA/JPL: p. 23; Shahram Sharifi: p. 12.

Library and Archives Canada Cataloguing in Publication

Title: Alien visitations / Louise Spilsbury.
Names: Spilsbury, Louise, author.
Description: Series statement: History raiders | Includes bibliographical references and index.
Identifiers: Canadiana (print) 20210192518 | Canadiana (ebook) 20210192526 | ISBN 9781427151025 (hardcover) | ISBN 9781427151087 (softcover) | ISBN 9781427151148 (HTML) | ISBN 9781427151209 (EPUB)
Subjects: LCSH: Unidentified flying objects–Sightings and encounters–Juvenile literature. | LCSH: Human-alien encounters–Juvenile literature. | LCSH: Extraterrestrial beings–Juvenile literature.
Classification: LCC TL789.2 .S65 2022 | DDC j001.942–dc23

Library of Congress Cataloging-in-Publication Data

Available at the Library of Congress

Crabtree Publishing Company

www.crabtreebooks.com 1-800-387-7650

 In Canada: We acknowledge the financial support of the Government of Canada through the Canada Book Fund for our publishing activities.

Published in Canada
Crabtree Publishing
616 Welland Ave.
St. Catharines, Ontario
L2M 5V6

Published in the United States
Crabtree Publishing
347 Fifth Ave
Suite 1402-145
New York, NY 10016

Printed in the U.S.A./062021/CG20210401

CONTENTS

ALIENS ON EARTH

One of the biggest questions humans ask is whether they are alone in the universe. Are there aliens somewhere out there in space? "Alien" is another word for extraterrestrial life-form. The word "extraterrestrial" means "outside Earth." But how can we know if aliens exist? And if they do, have they ever visited Earth?

Aliens in History

Scientists have yet to discover life beyond Earth. However, most believe that it exists. People have reported seeing unusual objects in the sky that could be alien spaceships. Others claim to have been kidnapped by aliens or contacted by extraterrestrials. Some people even believe that aliens have influenced ancient **civilizations**! For example, some people believe that the ancient Egyptians designed and built their **pyramids** with help from aliens.

In movies and TV shows, aliens are often shown as looking a little like humans. They usually have huge heads, huge eyes, and green, gray, or purple skin. However, the truth is, we don't know what aliens look like, if they do exist.

The universe is so huge that it is sensible to believe there could be alien life beyond Earth.

Explore History

In this book, we will journey across the world to discover where and when aliens may have visited Earth. As we do so, we will examine questions raised by these mysterious reports and try to answer them.

History Raider!

Hey! I'm Madison Maverick. I'm an explorer. I also like to think of myself as a history raider—a person who stops at nothing to find answers about the past. Come with me on my journeys to solve past mysteries and answer questions about history. Read my field notes on the History Raider pages and boxes. Then, jot down **evidence** to help solve each mystery.

ANCIENT ALIENS

Ancient civilizations built jaw-dropping structures and created innovative devices. But how was this possible without modern machinery? Were people in ancient civilizations helped by extraterrestrials?

Aliens in Egypt

There is some evidence that beings from outer space may have helped ancient civilizations. Historians have discovered 3,000-year-old **hieroglyphs** that seem to show a helicopter, an airplane, and a spaceship. People who believe in alien visitations argue that these images suggest that aliens visited Earth in ancient times. Why would the ancient Egyptians have created the images if they had not seen these objects in real life?

Unexplained in Rome

Several strange sightings were also recorded in ancient Rome. A famous Roman historian named Plutarch wrote of seeing a strange unexplained light in the sky. He described it as having "a huge, flame-like body." He wrote that it was shaped like a wine jar and had a silver color. Could this have been an alien spaceship flying above Earth?

Can you spot the spaceship, helicopter, and airplane images among these ancient Egyptian hieroglyphs? Could they be signs of ancient alien visitations?

The Nazca created designs in the desert sand, covering almost 190 square miles (492 sq km).

Aliens in the Desert?

Many people believe that aliens visited an ancient people called the Nazca. The Nazca lived in Peru, South America, from 100 B.C.E. to 800 C.E. Some people think that these designs, known as the Nazca lines, are evidence that aliens visited them long, long ago.

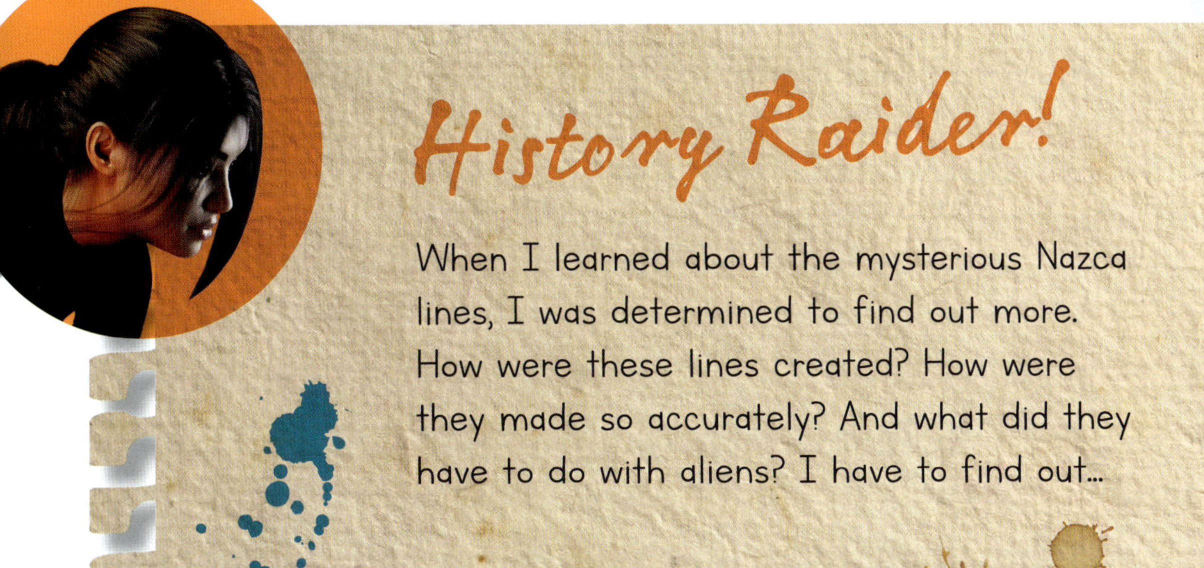

History Raider!

When I learned about the mysterious Nazca lines, I was determined to find out more. How were these lines created? How were they made so accurately? And what did they have to do with aliens? I have to find out...

History Raider! Lines in the Desert

As my plane circled above the mysterious Nazca lines, I could see why people think they were made by aliens. These 300 **geometric** shapes cover a vast area of **remote** Peruvian desert. Surely there's no way an ancient civilization like the Nazca could have drawn these images without being able to fly? I, too, began to wonder if aliens had been involved.

Investigating Clues

After I landed, my first stop was to check out some wooden **stakes** found by **archaeologists** near the carvings. I realized that the Nazca could have used them to scrape away the red stones that cover the land, revealing the white sand beneath. But how did they make the drawings so accurate?

Climbing for Answers

I braved the heat to climb one of the surrounding **foothills** to find the answer. There, on high ground, I clearly saw some of the lines below. Perhaps instructions to create the lines were sent from atop the foothills to people below. The instructions may have explained where to lay ropes to create outlines for the shapes. People could then have scraped perfect lines into the ground, guided by the ropes.

With so little wind and rain in the desert, the Nazca lines have stayed intact for around 2,000 years.

A Sign to the Gods?

At ground level, no one can clearly see the drawings. So who were they created for, and why? I knew that the Nazca lived in a very dry place, where it was difficult to grow crops. I also read that they worshiped gods and prayed to them for water. Perhaps the shapes were signs to the Nazca's gods, asking them for help. Some people even believe that the gods the Nazca worshiped were aliens! The lines may have been created so these extraterrestrial beings would see them from space! One thing is for sure—these enormous images were made so that someone, or something, could see them from above.

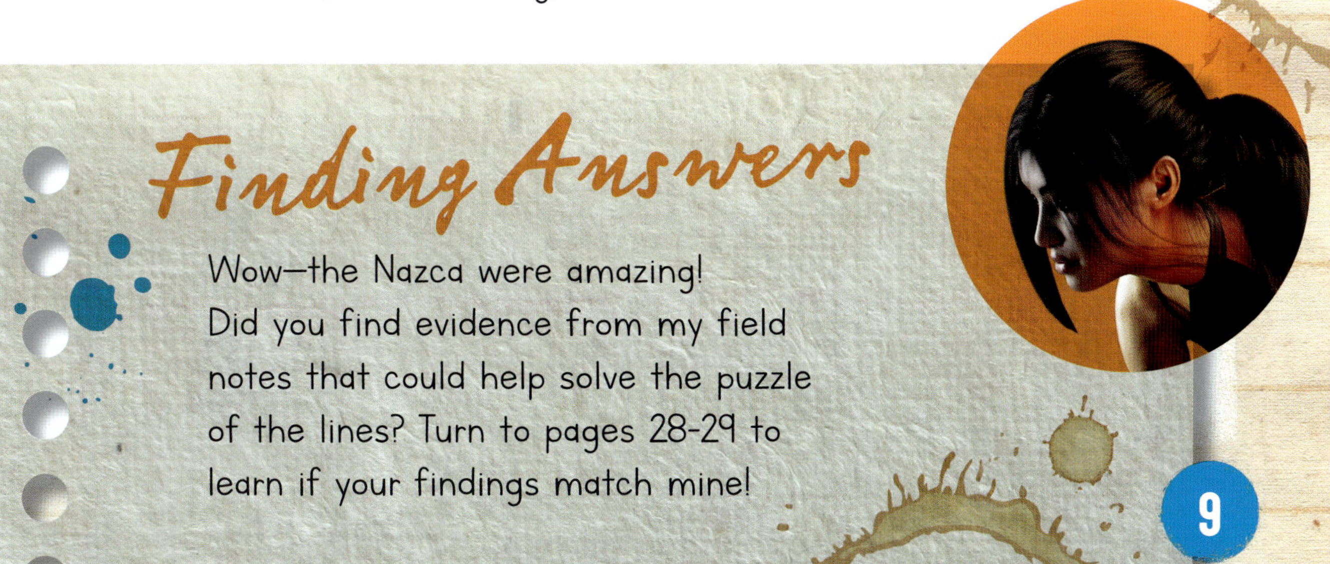

Finding Answers

Wow—the Nazca were amazing! Did you find evidence from my field notes that could help solve the puzzle of the lines? Turn to pages 28-29 to learn if your findings match mine!

MYSTERIOUS OBJECTS

Many people believe that aliens travel to Earth in mysterious unidentified flying objects, or UFOs. Although people have reported seeing UFOs since ancient times, these reports increased in the 1900s.

Flying Saucers

In 1947, an American pilot named Kenneth Arnold was flying near Mount Rainier in Washington. Suddenly he saw nine strange flying objects. He described them as moving incredibly fast and dipping in flight "like a **saucer** skipping on water." Although the U.S. military insisted there was no reason to believe they were alien spaceships, the sighting caught the public's imagination. Many more people claimed to see objects that looked like saucers in the sky. This led to the common term "flying saucers."

Project Blue Book

In the 1950s, the U.S. government set up a task force named "Project Blue Book." Its aim was to look into the sightings of flying saucers. The task force began to use the term "UFO" to mean something in the sky a person sees, but does not recognize. Project Blue Book found no evidence of alien spaceships.

This cloud hovering above Mount Rainier near Seattle, Washington, could easily be mistaken for a UFO!

Some people say that the increase in UFO sightings in the 1940s and '50s was because there were more aircraft in the sky during World War II (1939–1945). Soon after the war, air travel for tourism became popular.

Unsolved Mysteries?

Thousands of UFO sightings are reported every year around the world. Investigations usually find ordinary explanations for the strange sightings. They include bright stars, **meteors**, **artificial satellites**, and space junk burning up in Earth's **atmosphere**. However, mysteries still remain. There are some reported cases for which no logical explanation can be found. One famous example is from 1976, when a UFO was spotted over Tehran, Iran. Some claim it jammed the systems of two military jets that followed it.

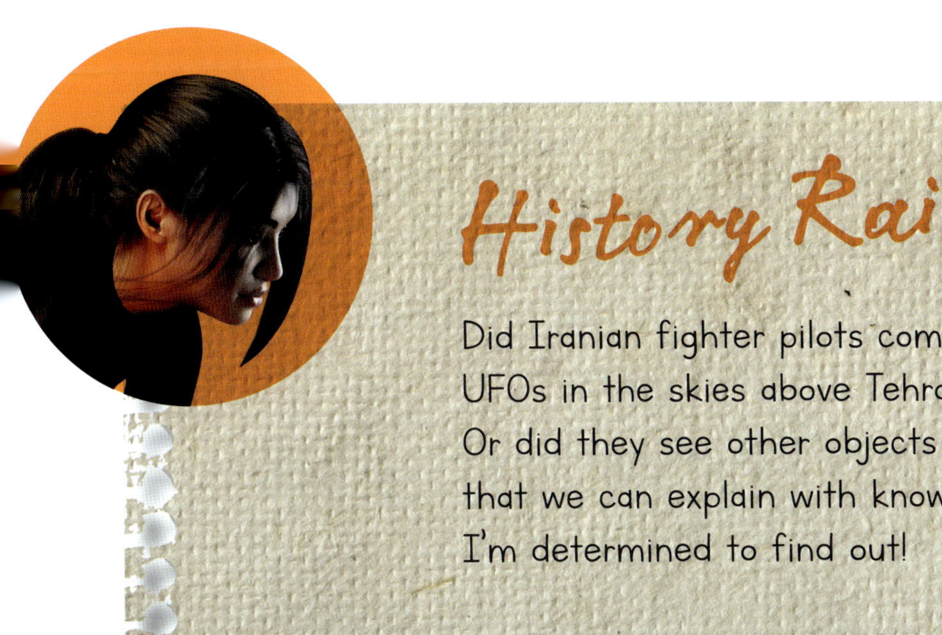

History Raider!

Did Iranian fighter pilots come across UFOs in the skies above Tehran in 1976? Or did they see other objects in the sky that we can explain with known science? I'm determined to find out!

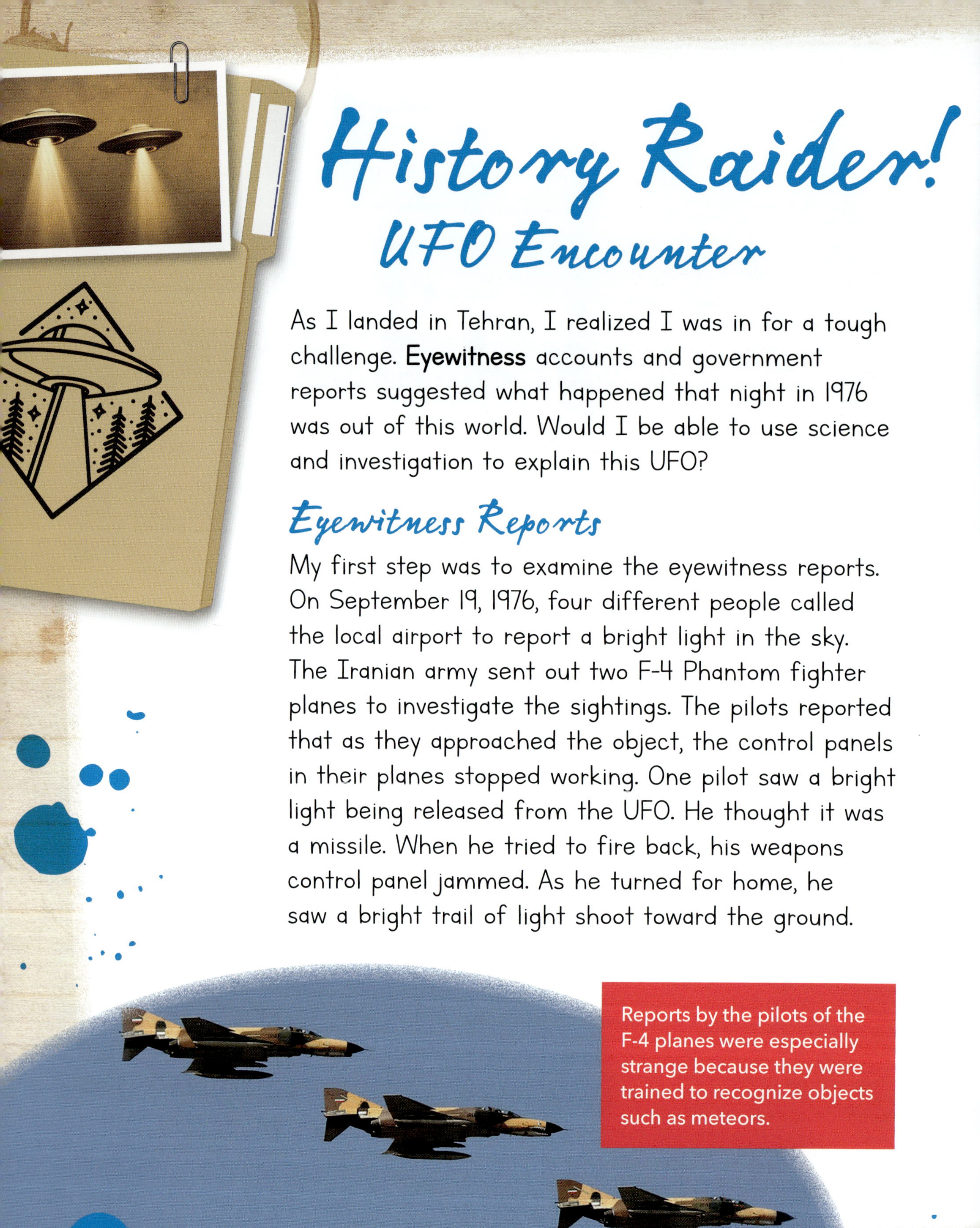

History Raider!

UFO Encounter

As I landed in Tehran, I realized I was in for a tough challenge. **Eyewitness** accounts and government reports suggested what happened that night in 1976 was out of this world. Would I be able to use science and investigation to explain this UFO?

Eyewitness Reports

My first step was to examine the eyewitness reports. On September 19, 1976, four different people called the local airport to report a bright light in the sky. The Iranian army sent out two F-4 Phantom fighter planes to investigate the sightings. The pilots reported that as they approached the object, the control panels in their planes stopped working. One pilot saw a bright light being released from the UFO. He thought it was a missile. When he tried to fire back, his weapons control panel jammed. As he turned for home, he saw a bright trail of light shoot toward the ground.

Reports by the pilots of the F-4 planes were especially strange because they were trained to recognize objects such as meteors.

Digging Deeper

That's where the story ended—with a lot of strange events, but no explanations. I hauled out my crate of star charts and investigated what else could have been in the sky that night. I discovered that the planet Jupiter would have been especially bright in the sky at that time. In fact, the people who first reported the UFO saw the light just where Jupiter would have been. The pilots and the other witnesses said the light was star shaped, so this could be a logical explanation.

Glowing Lights

The bright, glowing objects that shot toward the ground could be trails of meteors or space rocks left by a comet. But why did the jet controls start jamming? I spoke to an engineer who had worked on the aircraft. He admitted that the planes had experienced electrical problems before. Perhaps it was just a coincidence that they did so that night in 1976, too.

Finding Answers

This case is so mysterious! Did you find evidence that could help figure out what happened that night? Turn to pages 28-29 to learn if your findings match mine!

TAKEN BY ALIENS

Every year, there are many reports of people who claim to have been abducted, or kidnapped, by aliens. These people say that extraterrestrials took them into their alien spaceships to question or examine them.

Tall Tales?

Tales of alien abductions began in the 1800s. This was around the time that **airships** took to the sky. In one report, two men said three tall, slender, humanlike aliens with bodies covered in fine, soft hair tried to kidnap them. They said that they managed to escape. There has been a large increase in alien-abduction claims since the 1960s, when humans began to explore space in spaceships.

Once air travel began to take place in airships like these, stories started to be told about UFO sightings and alien abductions.

Stolen Hours

The tale of Betty and Barney Hill, from New Hampshire, is one of the most famous alien-abduction stories. The Hills claimed they were abducted by strange beings late one night in September 1961. They were on their way home from a vacation. They said they were taken on board a UFO where they were examined for two hours. The story was widely reported. It captured people's imagination so much that many later alien-abduction stories sounded very similar to theirs.

Some stories of alien abductions involved being taken up into UFOs by mysterious forces.

History Raider!

I'm fascinated by the Hills' story. They said they were followed down empty, winding roads by a strange white light. It looked like an object spinning in the air. They also said that after being abducted, the aliens erased their memories of the experience. They remembered their alien abduction only with the help of a psychiatrist (a medical doctor that deals with mental health). Could there be a **psychological** explanation for their experience? If so, what is it?

History Raider!

Alien Abduction

As I visited the spot where Betty and Barney Hill said the abduction happened, I felt a shiver down my spine. Their story was detailed and convincing. Could it be true that they were kidnapped and studied by aliens?

When Time Stopped...

The Hills said that when they arrived home, their watches had stopped working. There were two hours of the drive that neither one of them could remember. The only thing they remembered was seeing what they thought was a UFO. It was a metal disk the size of a house. They talked to a psychiatrist who helped them recall what happened that night.

Chatting with Aliens

The couple claimed the aliens examined them and took hair samples. Reports say that before the couple was returned to their car, Betty chatted to the aliens about where they came from.

The couple described their kidnappers. They were gray alien beings with spindly legs and large, catlike eyes.

Aboard a Flying Saucer?

The more reports I read, the more I became convinced that Betty and Barney were not knowingly lying. They truly believed their story. They were smart people who did not have a history of telling tall tales. But I wanted to delve deeper. I spoke to psychiatrists who had studied other abduction reports. They think the people involved were having **hallucinations**.

Can Science Explain?

I also learned about a scientific condition called sleep paralysis. This can happen when people are waking up or on the edge of falling asleep. It is reasonable that a person could experience sleep paralysis when tired and driving late at night, like the Hills were. During sleep paralysis, people feel aware, but they are unable to move or speak. They may feel like they are floating or flying, or that they have a heavy weight on their chest. They can also have hallucinations. These hallucinations can sometimes be very scary. Could Betty and Barney have experienced sleep paralysis that night in 1961? It could be an answer to this mystery.

Finding Answers

The Hills' story is so intriguing. Did you gather evidence that helps answer my questions about it? Turn to pages 28-29 to learn if your findings match mine!

CAPTURING ALIENS

As well as stories of aliens abducting humans, there have also been reports of people capturing and studying aliens. Some people believe that aliens have been caught so that they can be examined. They say that governments try to keep their discoveries a secret. According to them, that is why there are no stories about alien captures in the news.

A Secret Project

One of the most famous stories of alien capture is centered on Roswell in New Mexico. In 1947, newspapers said that a "flying saucer" had crashed nearby. The U.S. Air Force arrived and cleared up the crash. Years later, researchers interviewed witnesses. They said the area had been sealed off by armed soldiers and that a strange crashed craft was taken away. They also said that pieces of the craft were unlike any material produced on Earth. The researchers said that an alien spaceship had crashed at Roswell. Some evidence points to the fact that the U.S. government keeps alien technology, like the Roswell saucer, at Area 51—a military base in Nevada.

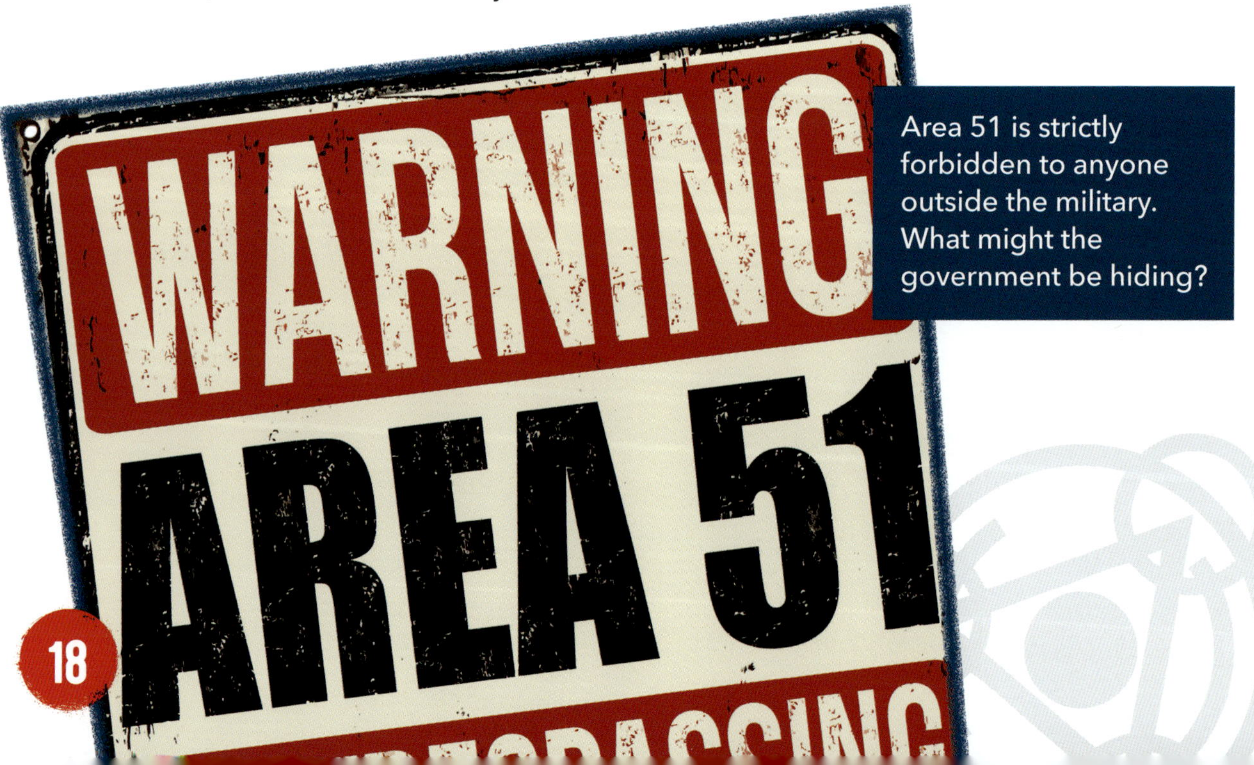

Area 51 is strictly forbidden to anyone outside the military. What might the government be hiding?

Many people still claim that an alien spacecraft crash-landed in an area near Roswell.

The Mystery of Hangar 18

Some people believe that the U.S. government has a secret warehouse in Dayton, Ohio. It is believed to be named Hangar 18. People claim there is evidence of alien captures and investigations hidden there. This evidence is said to include flying saucer debris, alien bodies, and even living captured aliens! The location is believed to be sealed tight and heavily guarded.

History Raider!

As soon as I read about the mysteries surrounding Area 51 and Roswell, I knew I had to find out the truth behind the headlines. What did the U.S. military have to do with the stories about UFOs and aliens? What were they trying to keep so secret? Had alien bodies been found or was there another explanation?

History Raider!

Alien Autopsy

Visiting Roswell and Area 51 was spooky. Immediately, I remembered images from a movie of an alien **autopsy**. It was supposed to have happened there and it made me feel very uneasy.

Evidence Emerges

I read newspaper stories about a UFO crash landing in 1947. Eyewitnesses claim they saw bodies of small, humanlike aliens being stored at the site. Over the years, the stories were almost forgotten. However, in 1995, a movie that seemed to show an autopsy of an alien body was released. It was seen all over the world. Was this proof that an alien autopsy really happened?

On the Case

I made some fascinating discoveries. There had been a cover-up! It seems that the U.S. Army first announced that a flying saucer had indeed crashed in the area. Then the army changed its story and said that, in fact, the wreckage was a **weather balloon**. Later, the army admitted both these stories were designed to hide the truth. The U.S. government said it told lies because it did not want the Russian government to know they had really been sending a spy device in the sky. The device was meant to discover if the Russians were testing **nuclear bombs**.

This is a model of an alien body. Could the Roswell alien have been created in a similar way?

Real or Fake?

What about that movie of the autopsy? The U.S. Army said that people did not see alien bodies taken from the site. They insisted the "bodies" people saw were just parachute dummies taken from test aircraft. I also tracked down an interview with the man who made the autopsy movie. He admitted that the movie was almost entirely fake. However, he still insisted that real footage existed. He claimed he had been forced to recreate it because the original movie was damaged. Maybe that is why some people feel that all the questions surrounding Roswell have not been answered yet.

Finding Answers

My research into Area 51 was chilling. I made notes of all the evidence I found that could help solve this mystery. Did you? Turn to pages 28-29 to learn if your findings match mine!

LOOKING FOR ALIENS

Today, people are using science to search for aliens. The search for extraterrestrial intelligence is known as SETI. It takes place at observatories **here on Earth, where scientists look for signs of intelligent life on other worlds. New technologies are also sent into space to look for aliens.**

Sweeping the Skies

On Earth, scientists use giant **radio telescopes** that listen for beeps, squeaks, and any other signs of alien activity in space. The telescopes can detect signals, such as the flash of a distant powerful **laser**. In 2020, a radio telescope detected signals from a **galaxy** far away. The signals were released in a regular 16-day pattern. The regular signals suggest they might have been made by intelligent life.

Messages to Space

Space **probes** are robot spacecraft that can travel far into distant space. In 1977, the National Aeronautics and Space Administration (NASA) launched two probes–*Voyager 1* and *Voyager 2*–to study the planets in the **solar system**. Aboard the *Voyager* probes there are golden **records** that contain pictures, sounds, and words in different languages. If living things from another planet find the probes, the records will tell them about Earth and its people.

These giant telescopes at the Very Large Array (VLA) observatory in New Mexico, United States, are used for SETI.

Space Exploration

A range of amazing technologies has been sent into space to search for alien life. For example, *Curiosity* is a type of vehicle called a rover. It has moved across the surface of Mars. It discovered rounded pebbles that show water once flowed on Mars. *Curiosity* also detected chemicals that are necessary for life. Space probes and radio telescopes have recently discovered that some of the moons that **orbit** other planets in the solar system have icy oceans. The water there could hold alien life.

The *Voyager* probes set off in 1977. They have traveled farther than any other humanmade object.

History Raider!

The idea of alien life beneath icy oceans in space definitely sparked my interest. If alien life is living in these icy worlds, what might it look like? And how would it survive in these challenging places? My next mission was to find out more!

History Raider!

Alien Animals Alert!

I'd heard rumors that space oceans might contain **bacteria**. Some people think that animals similar to Earth's fish could feed on the bacteria. In turn, those animals might be **prey** for larger space beasts. What would these alien animals look like? Could they really exist? I needed to find out whether this was a far-fetched fantasy or if it could be true...

Probing Further

I tracked down facts from the *Cassini-Huygens* space probe mission. It explored Saturn and took pictures of Jupiter from 2000 to 2019. The pictures and information the probe collected were incredible. On Enceladus, Saturn's sixth-largest moon, it found signs of hydrothermal vents on the moon's ocean floor. Hydrothermal vents are holes in an ocean floor that let out heat and chemicals. In Earth's oceans, bacteria get energy to live from these vents. If the vents exist on Enceladus, it is possible this could happen there, too.

The *Cassini* spacecraft spotted jets of steam and tiny pieces of ice shooting out from Enceladus's underground ocean. This tells us there could be hydrothermal vents on the moon's ocean floor.

Ocean Life?

I also discovered that Jupiter's moon, Europa, may contain more liquid water than all of Earth's oceans combined. This water—and any life in it—is protected by a thick layer of ice that is miles deep. So far, no spacecraft have visited or collected images from below the ice. However, it seems that the ingredients for life could be there, too.

Future Finds?

If there is life in these oceans, the experts I spoke to think it will be living things that are too small to see without a microscope. But for 90 percent of Earth's history, the only life on the planet was tiny living things like bacteria. So, even if there are no ocean animals in space now, some people believe there could be in the future.

Maybe alien ocean life will be bioluminescent, like some ocean life on Earth. Bioluminescent means to glow in the dark.

Finding Answers

I've learned so much about alien life and where we might find it. My notebook is full of information. Have you recorded evidence, too? Turn to pages 28-29 to learn if your findings match mine!

ONGOING MYSTERIES

Discovering whether or not we are alone in the universe is a fascinating idea. So, too, is the thought that there might be other planets or moons where humans could live one day. The universe is massive, and many planets are too far away to be discovered by today's technology. How will people find them? And will finding faraway planets lead to the discovery of alien life?

Eyes in Space

There are so many planets, moons, and other objects to explore that powerful future telescopes might be the best hope of discovering alien life. Telescopes in space can scan the skies to find Earth-sized planets. They can also detect planets beyond the solar system, which have never been explored before. Scientists believe these planets are the most likely to hold alien life.

The James Webb Space Telescope

Future space telescopes will not just see things. They will be able to study the atmospheres, seasons, and even surfaces of faraway worlds. The James Webb Space Telescope (JWST) will also be able to sense warmth. This will allow it to spot planets and moons that have surfaces warm enough for life. It will have the ability to detect chemicals in the atmospheres of distant planets and moons, to find out which ones have the ingredients for life.

Could the mirrors of the amazing JWST detect alien life in the future?

In the future, a robot submarine craft may carry out detailed scientific investigations under the surface of a Kraken, a sea on Saturn's moon Titan.

Space Submarines

Scientists and inventors are already hard at work designing a robot submarine that will be able to explore space oceans beneath distant moons. The first will attempt to drill through deep layers of ice to discover what lies beneath the surface of the seas on the biggest of Saturn's 82 moons: Titan. Scientists are interested in Titan because it has a surface similar to Earth's, with lakes and seas and possibly an underground ocean, too. The seas there however, are not filled with water but with chemicals. If a space submarine works, similar future submarines would be able to look for life in the mysterious underwater worlds of moons like Europa and Saturn's Enceladus.

History Raider!

For adventurers like us, space is full of mysteries and wonders to explore. The history of alien visitations has been so much fun to explore, and raids into the future look just as exciting!

MYSTERY SOLVED?

Some of those mysteries were pretty spooky, weren't they? After gathering the evidence, here are some conclusions I made after each journey. How do yours match up?

Pages 8-9: Lines in the Desert

The Nazca could have made the lines without extraterrestrial help. They may have used wooden stakes to create the lines. People may have stood on hills to show workers where to lay lines of rope to make the lines. The lines may have been signs to the Nazca's gods.

Pages 12-13: UFO Encounter

Though the events in Tehran are strange, there are likely explanations. Jupiter would have been visible in the sky, which could explain the lights. The lights could also have been a comet or space junk burning.

Pages 16-17: Alien Abduction

The Hills seemed to recount a true experience. However, they may have suffered sleep paralysis and seen, heard, and felt the abduction because they were hallucinating.

Pages 20-21: Alien Autopsy

Area 51 has had some mysterious occurrences. However, there is limited evidence of alien testing there. It is likely that the U.S. Army lied about the wreckage to keep secret its military operations against Russia. The bodies may simply have been parachute dummies. There is no true footage of an alien autopsy.

Pages 24-25: Alien Animals Alert!

No one has yet visited the icy oceans in which scientists believe there may be alien life. Scientists have suggested that if there is life, it could be in the form of bacteria—which in turn could be food for bigger life, including alien sharks. The possible existence of hydrothermal vents on Enceladus point to the existence of bacteria in space. Even if larger alien animals do not exist now, they could in the future.

GLOSSARY

airships Lighter-than-air aircraft

archaeologists People who study history through evidence

artificial satellites Humanmade objects that orbit Earth

atmosphere Layers of gases that surround planets and moons

autopsy An examination of a body after death

bacteria Very tiny living things

civilizations Settled and organized groups of people

evidence A sign that shows something exists or is true

eyewitness Describes an account told by a person who has seen something

foothills Low hills at the base of mountains

galaxy A group of millions of stars, dust, and gas

geometric A pattern of regular shapes

hallucinations Things that appear real, but are created by a person's mind

hieroglyphs Ancient Egyptian writing that used pictures instead of letters

laser A device that produces a very narrow and powerful beam of light

meteors Rocklike objects that travel through space and glow when they enter a planet's atmosphere

nuclear bombs Explosive devices that use nuclear reactions to cause explosions

observatories Buildings with large telescopes

orbit When one object in space goes around another object

prey An animal that is hunted and eaten by other animals

probes Unmanned spacecraft that explore the solar system and send information back to Earth

psychological Related to the mind and emotions

pyramids Large structures that have a square base and four triangular sides

radio telescopes Telescopes that use radio signals to learn about faraway objects

records Round disks on which sounds and images have been recorded

remote Far away from places where people live

saucer A small, round, shallow dish to hold a cup

solar system The Sun and the planets in orbit around it, including Earth

stakes Wooden rods or poles

weather balloon A balloon that floats high to collect information about the weather

BOOKS

Galat, Joan Marie. *Absolute Expert: Space: All the Latest Facts from the Field.* National Geographic Kids, 2020.

Gater, Will. *The Mysteries of the Universe*. DK Children, 2020.

Hawksett, David. *Extraterrestrials: Can You Find Them in the Universe?* (Be a Space Scientist). PowerKids Press, 2018.

O'Brien, Cynthia. *Searching for Extraterrestrials* (Mission: Space Science). Crabtree Publishing, 2019.

WEBSITES

Read more about exploring space at:
www.esa.int/kids/en/learn/Life_in_Space/Exploration/Space_Exploration

Find out more about aliens and alien life at:
https://kids.britannica.com/kids/article/alien/399331

Learn more about exoplanets–planets in space that might support life–at:
https://exoplanets.nasa.gov/alien-worlds

Learn more about Titan and alien seas at:
https://kids.nationalgeographic.com/explore/space/alien-sea

INDEX

About the Author

Award-winning author Louise Spilsbury, who also writes under the name Louise Kay Stewart, has written more than 250 books for young people on a wide range of exciting subjects. When she's not tapping away at the computer keys, Louise loves swimming in the sea and making bonfires on the beach near her home.